No Proof Needed

The Bible is the Word of God

Dr. Charles R. Vogan Jr.

Ravenbrook Publishers

Ravenbrook Publishers

A subsidiary of
Shenandoah Bible Ministries

www.shenbible.org

ISBN 978-0-6151-3938-8

Copyright © 2002 Charles R. Vogan Jr.
All rights reserved

Scripture taken from the HOLY BIBLE, NEW INTERNATIONAL VERSION, Copyright © 1973, 1978, 1984 International Bible Society. Used by permission of Zondervan Bible Publishers.

Contents

Introduction	5
Revelation	14
The Word of Prophecy	27
Witnesses	39
God Uses Man	51
A Book for Faith	61
Unbelief	70
Conclusion	80

Introduction

The Bible has been around for a long time, longer than any culture or people in our modern society can remember. It predates us all. Though every culture and historical period has tried to leave its impression on the Bible – versions, translations, manuscripts, as well as edicts against it and governments outlawing it, textbooks and "pop culture" books trying to make it more acceptable to modern man – it has remained, like a rock, unchanged through all the attempts to modify it, deny it, and force it to fit with our own world views. And when we are weary of life and pass on, the Bible will still be here teaching the same message to those who follow after us.

So it seems pretty arrogant that people casually call God a liar about his own book.

> Anyone who does not believe God has made him out to be a liar, because he has not believed the testimony God has given about his Son. (1 John 5:10)

The Bible claims to be God's Word.[1] This means, at the simplest level, that **God spoke these words** through man. It is not a production of brilliant religious Jews, but a work in spite of

---

[1] The number of references to this idea in the Bible are too numerous to list here; my personal favorite is Paul's statement to the Thessalonians – "And we also thank God continually because, when you received the *Word of God*, which you heard from us, you accepted it not as the word of men, but as it actually is, the *Word of God*, which is at work in you who believe." (1 Thessalonians 2:13) He is commending them for believing that the Bible really is the Word of God and not falling prey to the doubts that many have about it.

them. They would not have known these truths if God had not told them. *God* has spoken; the Bible comes from outside the world; it is *revelation*.

Second, if the Bible is the Word of God, then it is **authoritative**. If God really wrote this book, then we *must* listen to it – we ignore it at our peril. Our God is speaking to us, not just another human! These are issues that only God can address; we won't find them explained anywhere else, and they pertain to the welfare of our souls – and our relationship with the Creator and King of the universe. We will one day have to give an account to him for what we've heard from the Bible.

Third, if the Bible is the Word of God, then it is the ***truth***. God by definition would have the best and only true insight into the world, even of the mind of man. It is the standard by which all other "truths" are judged. If there is ever a conflict between God's truth and man's truth, then man's "truth" is suspect; God is never wrong, or inaccurate, or insufficient for our needs.

These three points force us to take a serious look at the Bible's claims. If the Bible really is the Word of God, then we cannot ignore it. We must begin studying it and finding out what it has to say to us. It's an integral part of our world.

If it weren't for sin, none of us would have a problem with the Bible. We would simply believe it, like Jesus' requirement of being like little children (Matthew 18:3), and profit by it. But God's book gets into our secret lives and uncovers disturbing things about us – we are full of sin, and we are rebels against God's rule and Law over us. We like depravity; we love the very things that God hates. We are more interested in our own glory and living for our own purposes, than for God's glory and will. These fatal character flaws are ingrained in every one of us to some degree. And the Bible turns the heat on, so to speak, by claiming that a person with these flaws can expect nothing good from God. Its teaching on this issue is very plain.

We can't just ignore these criticisms about us. If the Bible is true, then there are certain facts about God that are dangerous to ignore:

First, God claims to be our <u>Creator</u>. He made us a certain way, and he is saying in the Bible that we aren't operating according to his blueprints anymore. Wouldn't the architect know better than we would if things are going wrong? Wouldn't he know best what right and wrong are?

Second, God claims to be our <u>Judge</u>. He reserves the right (since he made us!) to decide what to do with a creation gone bad. Anyone who makes a machine that goes haywire has the right to change or even destroy the machine, if necessary, and start over. And the Bible claims that God has set up a special day in the future when he will review our performance and decide what to do with us – "For we must all appear before the judgment seat of Christ, that each one may receive what is due him for the things done while in the body, whether good or bad." (2 Corinthians 5:10)

This is where the Bible really comes through for us. Not only does it warn us of the trouble we are in, but also it shows us the way out of trouble. Nobody can claim that God hasn't given us fair warning! The directions for fixing our hearts and surviving Judgment Day are very clear and simple in the Bible; they are there for anybody to read, and there shouldn't be any problem following the steps. This is called "salvation." No wonder then that Jesus said, "The words I have spoken to you are spirit and they are life." (John 6:63)

But not everyone recognizes help when they see it. Our animosity toward God and his ways are deep-rooted. We have all developed ways of getting around the Bible's uncomfortable and accurate scrutiny of our hearts. Some of us simply read around the "negative" passages and we study those passages that are more "positive." That's like ignoring the tax collector and hoping he'll go away! This doesn't solve a thing, because until we pinpoint our spiritual illness and apply God's specific remedies to it, we can never be saved. As Jesus said, "I told you that you would die in your sins; if you do not believe that I am the one I claim to be, you will indeed die in your sins." (John 8:24) At the end of time, God is going to gather us together around his throne and judge us, whether we're ready or not.

Others of us take a more sinister approach – we accuse the Bible itself of being wrong. Our ally in this strategy is the devil himself; he has been casting doubt on the Word of God since the beginning (*"Did God really say . . .?"* – Genesis 3:1). This is the thinking: if we can show that the Bible really isn't God's Word, then that means that it's only the product of men and women. And though they certainly have the right to their opinions, I have the right to my opinions as well. Who is to say that they know the "truth" and others don't? Who can prove that they were "right" and I'm wrong in how I view the world, or in how I want to live my life?

So once a person has eliminated the Bible as the sole authority in matters of religion and morality, then he is free to choose his own authority – his own God, so to speak. The Bible then becomes an interesting relic from the past, no more than a record of how the Israelites chose to worship their God. And he then becomes free to choose his own way of worshipping his God. If that entails a little borrowing from the Bible here and there, why not? We choose interesting principles to live by from Confucius and Shakespeare too! But mainly what many people insist on is the right to cut out parts of the Bible that they don't like.

A clever strategy, but it won't work. Its weakness is that people are conveniently overlooking some massive realities in the Bible. It's our purpose here to point out some of those realities and put the lie to the devil's scheme. The Bible really is the Word of God, and we really do have to take it seriously. It's a shame that people are going to have to learn that the hard way on Judgment Day, but they will.

Is there any proof for the claim that the Bible is the Word of God? *No* – there is no proof whatever for this claim. The Bible doesn't need proof. In fact, it gives us very little proof of its divine origin because *the Bible is a kind of document that doesn't require proof.* Its plain statement of the truth is sufficient to analyze us, judge us, condemn us and save us. All we're supposed to do is believe, not doubt.

What it amounts to is this: we have one opportunity to accept the Bible on its bare word, because the next time we will hear this truth is on Judgment Day when it's too late to do anything about it! Only *then* will we get the "proof" that we were insisting on. Right now, however, God has decided to publish his truth that you can accept or reject *without proofs* (he did this deliberately, for various reasons). Those who accept it will be rewarded with its promises *at the end of time* (see Hebrews 11:13, 39-40), and those who reject it will discover their mistake *only at the end of time*.

One reason the Bible doesn't need proof is that we know already that it's true. Our loud demands that we're not going to believe it until someone proves it to us is a cover-up. We know that God has perfectly described our hearts in the Bible, and that we are obligated to serve him, and that we've failed him. We know that he has the answer to life. Our own hearts testify to us that we are sinners. We just don't want to listen or do things on God's terms. Paul accurately described the typical sinner:

> The wrath of God is being revealed from Heaven against all the godlessness and wickedness of men who **suppress** the truth by their wickedness, since what may be known about God is **plain to them**, because God has **made it plain** to them. For since the creation of the world God's invisible qualities – his eternal power and divine nature – have been **clearly seen**, being **understood** from what has been made, so that men are **without excuse**. For although they **knew** God, they neither glorified him as God nor gave thanks to him, but their thinking became futile and their foolish hearts were darkened. (Romans 1:18-21)

So the problem is not about whether we *can* know the truthfulness of the Bible, but whether we *want* to know it. It's not a philosophical problem but a moral one. It doesn't require intelligence (even the ignorant can understand its point) but your **will**.

God's people know that the Bible is true without anybody proving it to them. In Christianity we call this accepting the Bible by **faith**, not by sight. The reason we have to rely on *spiritual* insight to use the Bible is because there is nothing in this world that can possibly be used to prove the Bible – as we've seen in generations of Bible students trying and failing to impress atheists with various well-meant arguments. Faith, however, is a gift from God (Ephesians 2:8) – it's the ability to see beyond the darkness and confusion in this world into God's world. With faith it's easy to see that the Bible is God's Word; no further proof is necessary. Without faith, there is no proof possible.

Some would accuse us of using the impossible to prove the impossible here. Isn't it convenient, critics would say, that one needs faith to understand the Bible – and only God gives a person that faith! They're not impressed with arguments that leave them on the outside, and only the selected few on the inside understand the mysteries. It smacks too much of self-delusion.

But again, we can't ignore some of the major characteristics of the Bible. The Bible is designed in such a way that it doesn't need any proofs. God's purpose was not to convince the skeptics but to convict the sinner and save those who go to him for help. It's not a book to be proven, but a manual to be used. It's not for the unbelievers primarily but for the believers. It definitely has something to say to the unbelievers, but it certainly isn't going to submit itself to their approval. For them it is only a challenge and a threat from Heaven: repent and believe, or die in your sins!

The burden of proof is on the critic, not on the Bible – and certainly not with Christians! It's not our job to prove the Bible, simply to declare it to our generation. If they don't believe it, then obviously God isn't giving them the faith to see it – and we simply move on. It takes two to make a convert: the one who preaches, and God who opens the eyes to see. This is why we pray whenever we preach: we ask God to do his part to make our part work.

> How, then, can they call on the one they have not believed in? And how can they believe in the one of whom they have not heard? And how can they hear without someone preaching to them? And how can they preach unless they are sent? As it is written, "How beautiful are the feet of those who bring good news!" (Romans 10:14-15)

When the disciples failed to win converts in a certain town, they wanted something catastrophic to happen to that town to wake them up. But Jesus took the wiser approach: "If anyone will not welcome you or listen to your words, shake the dust off your feet when you leave that home or town. I tell you the truth, it will be more bearable for Sodom and Gomorrah on the Day of Judgment than for that town." (Matthew 10:14-15) Notice that he leaves the "proof" of the message till Judgment Day.

Besides, as we've seen before, there is nothing that we can do to "prove" the Bible to someone. Yet it's still our goal that a person believes that it really is God's Word. How can we reach our goal without trying to prove that it's true? Simply put, we can't; only the Holy Spirit can convince a person that this book is directly from God.

> I tell you the truth, no one can see the Kingdom of God unless he is born again. (John 3:3)

So we do our part – which is to *declare* (or preach, or teach) the Word of God – and we let God do his part – which is to convict, convince, and convert the heart.

Once people see that it's the Word of God, then they are in the perfect position to get the most out of the Bible. They will be open to the treasures of Heaven, the saving influence of Christ to deliver them from their sins, the protection of the Lord against the world's degenerating forces, and so much more. The Bible is the open door to all this treasure. But it only works for those who have a mind-transforming enlightenment as to the true nature of the Bible.

> Do not conform any longer to the pattern of this world, but be transformed by the renewing of your mind. Then you will be able to test and approve

what God's will is — his good, pleasing and perfect will. (Romans 12:2)

Revelation

The Bible is the revelation of God. To truly understand the nature and purpose of the Bible, we have to fully understand this point.

"Revelation" means an unveiling, an uncovering, so that we can see what has been formerly hidden. An artist will keep his work hidden until he's ready to unveil it to public view. The important point to make is that nobody can know what is hidden under the veil until the artist removes the veil – he alone knows what's behind it.

In the same way, there is a great deal of information *behind* the physical universe that was hidden from our view until God showed it to us in the Bible. There's a spiritual world behind the scenes that not only interacts with the physical world but upholds it and provides a framework for its activities. The mind of man is incapable of discovering anything about this spiritual world. If we are to know anything about it, God must pull away the veil and show us.

And now that we have the Bible, we need help interpreting it. Even the plain and simple words of the Revelation are going to be a mystery to us if God doesn't lead us by the hand through this strange world of his. That's why Bible study is never-ending, and the Bible will always be full of new things for us to discover. It's as simple or as deep as you want to go with it.

This is so different from what we are used to in our physical world that we can't seem to grasp the point. Scientists, for example, apply their minds to the physical universe and discover new things every day – without God's direct intervention. We are used to doing and thinking things on our own. Perhaps it makes us uncomfortable to rely on someone else leading us like a helpless baby. It's as if God is saying in the Bible, when it comes to the spiritual world of God you will always be helpless – you must never let go of my hand. You need me to show you every step of the way. As soon as you let go of me, you will go wrong.

There are several reasons for our helpless ignorance.

First, not long after man was created, he turned his back on God (in direct rebellion against God's command) and the connection between him and God was broken. We *used* to have a continual insight and awareness of the spiritual world (to better carry out our duties as God's administrators on earth). But now that insight and knowledge is gone. The relationship was broken, God withdrew himself into darkness, and now all that we are directly aware of is our physical universe.

Second, our hearts are steeped in rebellion and sin. Aside from the fact that God could hardly be expected to entrust his state secrets with perverted rebels and traitors, we typically turn everything we touch into suffering, ugliness, and death. We force the world to serve our own agendas, instead of finding out what God wants us to do with it. We can't be trusted with the simplest things anymore – we ignore God's instructions and commands, substitute our own in their place, and destroy the world in the process. We've created a real mess out of God's perfect world, as well as our own hearts! And though we think we can fix things, we're only fooling ourselves. The world's problems easily go from bad to worse in spite of our efforts.

Third, there is the very real problem of our physical outlook. We can only rely on our five senses to get around in the world. It's no wonder that atheists can get away with the challenge of "I don't see any God!" So when someone comes along with the Bible's story of a spiritual world behind the physical universe, of course that's going to be impossible to convince most people of without photographs and instrument readings.

Fourth, although we were designed with spiritual senses, they are dead now. The break with God at the beginning left us blind and deaf to the world of God. This shows up clearly when someone is confronted with the truth of God in the Bible and they don't see it. They can see the very words of God in cold print and it makes no impression on their hearts whatever. James told us that even the demons believe that there is a God – "and they shudder!" (James 2:19) But the same words have no effect on a sinner. If people could see God (the demons certainly can!) they would be terrified; but since they are blind spiritually, the idea of God is an empty phrase to them. "The man without the Spirit does not accept the things that come from the Spirit of God, for they are foolishness to him, and he cannot understand them, because they are spiritually discerned." (1 Corinthians 2:14)

So the first order of business is to learn who God is! In fact, the primary purpose of the Bible is to reveal God. All through the history of man, this question of the reality of God has been the biggest unknown. Is there a God? What is he really like?

> And without faith it is impossible to please God, because anyone who comes to him must believe that ***he exists*** and that he rewards those who earnestly seek him. (Hebrews 11:6)

Both philosophers and religions have attempted to answer this question, with the result that now we have no agreement among the philosophers on the nature of God, and there are multitudes of false gods on people's shelves and in their minds. This is inevitable when man is incapable of seeing the spiritual world of God. So to clear up the confusion once and for all, God took the veil away in the Bible, revealed himself, and now we know who he is.

There are two kinds of revelation: natural and special. "Natural" revelation consists of God's footprints, so to speak, that he left behind in the created world. This is what Paul meant when he said,

> The wrath of God is being revealed from Heaven against all the godlessness and wickedness of men who suppress the truth by their wickedness, since what may be known about God is plain to them, because God has made it plain to them. For since the creation of the world God's invisible qualities – his eternal power and divine nature – have been clearly seen, being understood from what has been made, so that men are without excuse. (Romans 1:18-20)

For example, we can tell that a ***wise*** God made the world because it works so well, like clockwork – everything has a place and a purpose. And we can tell that a ***just*** God made the world because we all know the importance of justice; governments use it, families use it. It's built into the fabric of the world and our hearts.

But it's still easy to deny that there's a God if one is determined to erase his footsteps from everything in sight. Sinners will deny even their own conscience in their desperate struggle to be free of God's rule over them. So scientists now claim that matter and energy have characteristics that naturally led everything to fit together efficiently; there was no God required. And conscience (we are told) is a cultural matter, a matter of taste – forcing everyone to adopt a moral standard that people lived by thousands of years ago is oppressive and unrealistic; it doesn't allow us the freedom to be ourselves.

So we can't really rely on natural revelation to learn about God; the image is blurry, our vision is marred, and our minds are too prone to reject even the plainest evidence. What we need is a simple statement, in language that we can understand, of what God is like. We need it in print, on paper, in words we are familiar with. What we need is called *special* revelation.

Special revelation is a written account in our own language. Language is one of the distinguishing features of humanity; we share physical senses with other creatures (in fact they often possess sharper and more efficient senses and physical abilities than we do!), but language is unique to us. I know that scientists like to think that dolphins and monkeys and other animals have their own "language;" but what I'm referring to is the verbal communication, through words and ideas, that human activity is based on. It's through this skill of ours that God chose to reveal the true nature of the spiritual world.

When God teaches us about himself through language, there's no reasonable way of getting it wrong. Now we can know exactly what God is like when he says of himself "God is Spirit."

(John 4:24) We now know that God is not animal, vegetable or mineral – he is not part of his own universe! In order to find God, we have to enter a *spiritual* world. The Bible is full of facts like this that eliminate all the false information that other religions have confused us with. It describes the real world of God in terms that are plain and simple to understand.

Not that he's going to explain everything to us! Some things he prefers to keep a mystery – such as, what exactly is "spirit?"

> The secret things belong to the LORD our God, but the things revealed belong to us and to our children forever, that we may follow all the words of this Law. (Deuteronomy 29:29)

But the information that he does reveal to us is going to be sufficient to head us off in the right direction if we want salvation from this God.

There are many things that we need to know about God, but without the Bible we can't possibly find out – which makes the Bible invaluable to us.

- **God himself** – The Bible tells us many profound things about God that will come in useful in times of need. For instance, what is God really like? Did he make the world? How did he do it? What is my relationship to him?

    God is a King, we learn, so that means the universe is his Kingdom and we are his subjects. God is a Judge; he measures the heart against the standard of his Law (which is spelled out very clearly) and rewards or punishes according to what he finds there. God is holy beyond anything else – a sinner must reconcile with this God or die, there are no two ways about it.

- **Man's spirit** – What is man, really? Why do we concern ourselves with the idea of God, and right and wrong, and eternity? The Bible shows us that we were made by God, in his image, to rule in his name over his Creation. We have a high calling! And this is why God is so interested in us.

- **Sin** – There are many definitions of sin in the world, and it seems that everyone has their own version to suit themselves. That would be handy if all we had was ourselves to please! But if there is a God, and if he has his own standards that he expects us to live by, it would be reasonable to assume that "sin" is breaking *his* rules, not our own.

    And in fact that's what the Bible tells us. The revelation of God shows us plainly what he expects of us, what we did wrong, and why it is wrong. The Law of God is a full and complete description of sin; any other version of right and wrong is man's imagination. Sin is, in short, rebellion against God's plain commands. "Sin is lawlessness." (1 John 3:4)

- **Our desperate situation** – Sin has put us in a desperate position of danger, and nobody knew that until God graciously warned us about it in the Bible. He could have kept this information hidden from us, but it was his intention all along to save some from the disaster that is looming over the whole world. So he pulled the veil away and showed us his wrath against unrepentant sinners, the eternal punishment of the wicked, the hardness of the human heart and the impossibility of anybody saving themselves on Judgment Day.

- **Jesus** – In keeping with God's plan to save a few, he sent his own Son (did we know he even *had* a Son until the Bible revealed this to us?) to work out the process of salvation. But one of the requirements of the process was that Jesus come incognito – nobody could tell, by looking at him, who he was or what he was doing here. Even the process of finding Jesus now, and closing with him, trusting him, and becoming one with him, is revealed only in the Word. Again, the Bible has to uncover the truth about Jesus so that we can see and believe, and be saved.

- **A new world in the making** – Man ruined (and is ruining!) the world that God first made. God could have destroyed the entire thing right at the beginning and started over (in fact, he showed his ability to destroy us, if he wanted to, through the Flood). But instead he began laying the foundations of a new world in which man can live a perfect life, free from sin and death, enjoying God directly, forever. It's an elaborate project that he is still working on – in fact, Christians are being built into it like stones in a wall. Someday the project will be complete and he will unveil the finished Temple, a house in which he intends to live with his people. The Bible contains the plans for this new world.

- **The demise of the old world** – While God makes a new world for his resurrected people to live in, he is laying plans to destroy this old world. It just isn't suitable for eternity; it won't meet the new spiritual needs of God's redeemed people. Scientists think that the universe is just going to wind down eventually and stop; they're wrong. God has decided to destroy the world completely, through fire, so that all traces of our familiar three-dimensional world (along with time) will disappear.

What a revelation! We would have known none of this if God had not shown us in the Bible what is happening right under our noses. Without this prior warning, we would have been caught unawares – death, and Judgment Day, would have surprised us with new realities that we didn't know existed. Now, however, we can know exactly what's going on in God's spiritual world – and read the "news" before it happens.

There's one more step to revelation, however, before we can fully appreciate how God uses the Bible. The facts in the Bible are true whether we believe them or not; they were written by God so that we would have fair warning about what is around us and ahead of us. If we don't believe it, it's not his fault! He plainly stated the facts; both those who act on them and those who don't will find out at the end that the Bible was true and complete in what it needed to show us about salvation.

The problem is that there are many that don't believe the Bible. And here is where we see the futility of trying to "prove" the Bible. The Bible deals with realities from another world; they can't be known through our normal senses, they are difficult to understand, we don't like them (being sinners, the holy bothers us!), and therefore the natural reaction is to discount the whole thing as myths and children's stories.

Step Two (which God had planned all along, because he knew man wouldn't be able to sense spiritual realities on his own even when so plainly laid out in simple language) is to make man's heart alive spiritually. The Spirit of God gives life to our spirits so that we can live – which, according to Jesus, is the ability to *know* God.

> Now this is eternal life: that they may **know** you, the only true God, and Jesus Christ, whom you have sent. (John 17:3)

This "knowing" means a real experience of God, meeting him, an encounter. The impossible happens: a human being who was heretofore cut off from ever knowing God now actually meets God, as a man meets a man. His spirit is alive to the sights and sounds of Heaven. The things that the Bible talks about become real to him; he can sense them, feel them, know them through his spirit – as he was designed to do in the beginning.

This step is just as much a revelation as the first step of the written Word, and just as necessary. "But if Christ is in you, your body is dead because of sin, yet your spirit is alive because of righteousness." (Romans 8:10) "Taste and see that the LORD is good." (Psalm 34:8)

> I will give them a heart to know me, that I am the LORD. They will be my people, and I will be their God, for they will return to me with all their heart. (Jeremiah 24:7)

Step Two doesn't always happen. When Noah was building his ark, he certainly told his neighbors what was going on. That was the initial revelation that he himself received from God – the warning of the coming wrath of God. But notice that only Noah and his family entered the ark; nobody else had the faith that Noah had, and so they died.

The Prophets were always struggling with unbelieving Israelites. "This is what the LORD says" punctuated their entire message; but though the people heard the very words of God, they didn't believe it and so they died. God eventually destroyed both the Northern and Southern Kingdoms for obstinately closing their hearts to the plain message of the Prophets.

Jesus made the message of salvation as clear as he could – and few believed him. He graphically described the misery of the wicked, the steps of salvation from sin, the glory of God, the heart of the sinner, and the former mysteries of the Kingdom. And the same people who heard that Word eventually crucified him for it!

The disciples, however, were filled with the Spirit (see Acts 2) and were awakened spiritually to understand the message of Christ. Once they saw it, once they met the God that Jesus was talking about, their lives were changed forever. They threw themselves into extending this kingdom which they had not understood or valued before. They weren't any more special, or privileged, or skilled, than their contemporaries; the difference was that the Holy Spirit made it real to them. They walked in the very presence of God.

And this is where we come into the picture. Modern Christians have received the Spirit of God and now they see and know the truths that the Apostles and Prophets saw.

> It was revealed to them that they were not serving themselves but you, when they spoke of the things that have now been told you by those who have preached the gospel to you by the Holy Spirit sent from Heaven. Even angels long to look into these things. (1 Peter 1:12)

Now let's stop and check where we are. The Bible is **revelation** – which means that God is showing us things that we didn't know, nor would we ever be able to figure them out on our own. No wisdom in the world, no tools or skills or powers, can pull out the mysteries hiding behind the physical universe. But we need this information desperately. It's partly because of our ignorance of these spiritual realities that we continually fail, are frustrated, and are burdened with sin and death.

The very things that we need to know about God, our souls, and the way to be saved from sin and death are plainly laid out for us in our own language in the Bible. There is no mistake now about the answer to the question, "what must we do to be saved?" Until God showed us we had no idea; now we have the true and simple answer. But even now the point will be lost on us unless God awakens our souls and makes us aware of him, his immensity and holiness and power, and our spiritual predicament. We have to feel the danger; we must see and long for the answer as a thirsty man longs for the water he sees at a distance.

I hope you can see from all of this that there is no way to *prove* any of this to someone. By the very nature of the thing, the Bible is not provable; nothing in this world can verify something that came from another, different world! All of our scientific instruments are designed to aid our five senses; but nobody can know God with their senses! It requires a spiritual life and awareness of the soul, and for that we have nothing to help us.

But then a proof wouldn't mean anything anyway, since the truth of the Bible can't be grasped until there's been a spiritual awakening in the soul. That only comes by means of the Spirit. So God doesn't offer any proofs of his revelation, nor does he expect his people to try to come up with any in the face of the critics. When he so desires he makes someone immediately aware of the truth of the Bible without our help.

God reveals himself – he relies on nothing else, he will accept help from no one else. "He saw that there was no one, he was appalled that there was no one to intervene; so his own arm worked salvation for him, and his own righteousness sustained him." (Isaiah 59:16) Wouldn't people always doubt a proof anyway? People can "prove" just about anything they want. But if God himself shows up in person, who needs proofs? The *reality* of God is all the proof we need.

The Word of Prophecy

It is through the Prophets that the entire Bible has come from God to us. He chose specific men to be the conduit, so to speak, for his Word. So the question of the Prophets has been the major battleground for whether the Bible is really the Word of God.

A prophet in Israel was not quite like prophets from other cultures, certainly not like the "prophets" that we moderns think of. What usually comes to mind is more like a fortuneteller – someone claims to be able to see into the future. But although the Israelite Prophets did know about, and proclaim, future events, that isn't what made them a prophet.

We also tend to use the word to describe an aggressive preacher, one who "gets in our faces" with the truth. The Prophets also did that, but again that falls short of what made a Biblical prophet. If being able to foretell the future and aggressively confronting people with a message are all the qualifications that we need for a true prophet, then certainly there are many prophets in our own day.

But the Prophets of the Bible were called to a unique job. We can best describe it by going back to the past and watching a battle shaping up between two kingdoms. If a king took his army to the field to invade another kingdom, he would often send a messenger ahead of the army to meet with the representatives of the other kingdom. That messenger was charged with the duty of relaying the king's exact words – surrender, or else be destroyed! The king trusted the messenger to deliver the warning faithfully, because a lot hung in the balance. If the other king took the hint, there would be no battle; the war was over, the new king would take over, and peace would ensue. But if the king proved to be defiant, then certainly there would be war.

So the messenger had to make sure of two things: first, that he got the message right, and second, that he faithfully relayed that message between the two kings. He was not to interfere at all with the message; too many lives depended on it being the very words and intent of the king himself.

The prophets of Israel did just that. The Israelites and their kings were supposed to be living by the Mosaic Law, but instead they followed the examples of their pagan neighbors and were not only living in immorality but also openly worshipping false gods! The time had come for the Lord – who was their rightful King – to assert his claim. So while amassing an "army" in Heaven (this is where his name "the LORD of Hosts" came from) he meanwhile sent a prophet ahead of the army to warn the Israelites: repent or die.

> Listen, a noise on the mountains, like that of a great multitude! Listen, an uproar among the kingdoms, like nations massing together! The LORD Almighty is mustering an army for war. (Isaiah 13:4)

> Who handed Jacob over to become loot, and Israel to the plunderers? Was it not the LORD, against whom we have sinned? For they would not follow his ways; they did not obey his law. So he poured out on them his burning anger, the violence of war. It enveloped them in flames, yet they did not understand; it consumed them, but they did not take it to heart. (Isaiah 42:24-25)

I myself will fight against you with an outstretched hand and a mighty arm in anger and fury and great wrath. I will strike down those who live in this city – both men and animals – and they will die of a terrible plague. After that, declares the LORD, I will hand over Zedekiah king of Judah, his officials and the people in this city who survive the plague, sword and famine, to Nebuchadnezzar king of Babylon and to their enemies who seek their lives. He will put them to the sword; he will show them no mercy or pity or compassion.' Furthermore, tell the people, 'This is what the LORD says: See, I am setting before you the way of life and the way of death. Whoever stays in this city will die by the sword, famine or plague. But whoever goes out and surrenders to the Babylonians who are besieging you will live; he will escape with his life. I have determined to do this city harm and not good, declares the LORD. It will be given into the hands of the king of Babylon, and he will destroy it with fire.' (Jeremiah 21:5-10)

It was the *message* that made the prophet, not just the things he did. It was a warning from God himself that unless the Israelites straightened out and returned to the Law, he was going to come in violence and justice and straighten them out the hard way.

The Prophets in the Old Testament are full of this message. Everywhere we look we find the messengers faithfully warning the rebels that God is coming with an army, and he is intent on setting up his own Kingdom over the ashes of man's distorted and perverted societies. For example, the famous passage of Isaiah 9 describes the kind of kingdom that Jesus is going to set up – and "the government will be on *his* shoulders" for a change.

The prophets came from the throne of God with their message. How would they know the crimes in the hearts of the people unless God the Judge, who sees the hearts of all, first showed them? How would they know God's plans unless they were there to witness the army that God was collecting together to destroy the wicked? How would they themselves escape the coming disaster if they dared to change the message of the King? If there's one thing that the King insists on, it is that the messenger faithfully relays his exact words to the people; he doesn't want anybody showing up before the throne of justice with the excuse that "your prophet didn't tell us that!"

> A wicked messenger falls into trouble, but a trustworthy envoy brings healing. (Proverbs 13:17)

Look anywhere in the Bible and you will see this theme over and over. John, for example, was brought into Heaven to witness the army that the Lord is amassing for that great day of judgment that is coming on all the earth.

> I saw Heaven standing open and there before me was a white horse, whose rider is called Faithful and True. With justice he judges and makes war. His eyes are like blazing fire, and on his head are many crowns. He has a name written on him that no one knows but he himself. He is dressed in a robe dipped in blood, and his name is the Word of God. The armies of Heaven were following him, riding on white horses and dressed in fine linen, white and clean. Out of his mouth comes a sharp sword with which to strike down the nations. "He will rule them with an iron scepter." He treads the winepress of the fury of the wrath of God Almighty. On his robe and on his thigh he has this name written: KING OF KINGS AND LORD OF LORDS. (Revelation 19:11)

Someone may charge that this is a hard interpretation of the Prophets – that it doesn't reflect the love of God that is so evident in the prophetic writings. But actually it's a realistic way of reading the Prophets. Remember two things: *first*, man is so desperately wicked, he is such a rebel against God, he has so offended God and the holy Law, that he and God are officially enemies now. This rebellion has to be broken first before we can talk about the positive aspects of God's Kingdom! There really are lines drawn between the two opponents and war is imminent.

Second, the very fact that God would send out a messenger before the battle is an act of mercy. This does show the heart of God. "He is patient with you, not wanting anyone to perish, but everyone to come to repentance." (2 Peter 3:9) The offer that he extends is simply amazing: repent, switch sides, surrender to me completely, and I will completely forgive you and make you one of my own. Only the King could make such a magnanimous offer to a rebel and traitor. Only God could have the kind of love that would accept a sinner into his family.

This is in fact the Gospel – the same message that Jesus himself preached. He was in fact the greatest of the Prophets, with an offer from the King in Heaven for all who would listen.

> "The time has come," he said. "The kingdom of God is near. Repent and believe the good news!" (Mark 1:15)

The entire Bible is prophecy, for that matter. Moses, through whom the Lord gave the Law and set up Israel as his personal Kingdom, was known as the greatest of the Old Testament prophets.

> Since then, no prophet has risen in Israel like Moses, whom the LORD knew face to face, who did all those miraculous signs and wonders the

LORD sent him to do in Egypt – to Pharaoh and to
all his officials and to his whole land. For no one
has ever shown the mighty power or performed
the awesome deeds that Moses did in the sight of
all Israel. (Deuteronomy 34:10-12)

And the power of his prophetic ministry was based on his closeness to God – he saw more of God's spiritual world than other prophets did.

When a prophet of the LORD is among you, I
reveal myself to him in visions, I speak to him in
dreams. But this is not true of my servant Moses;
he is faithful in all my house. With him I speak face
to face, clearly and not in riddles; he sees the form
of the LORD. Why then were you not afraid to speak
against my servant Moses? (Numbers 12:6-8)

After Moses came the other prophets who expounded and interpreted the Mosaic Law; in addition, they had their own dire warnings of "get this straight or else!" Then a prophet greater than Moses came – but again preaching a kingdom that would overwhelm the kingdoms of the earth.

The LORD your God will raise up for you a
prophet like me from among your own brothers.
You must listen to him. (Deuteronomy 18:15)

This second major prophet, Jesus, was followed by more "minor" prophets – the Apostles expounded and interpreted the message of Christ in their writings, plus added their own prophecies of the coming Kingdom at the end of time.

That means that the entire Bible was written by prophets who were charged with bringing God's message direct from his throne to us.

Now the prophets all claimed to have heard the voice of God; they repeatedly claimed that their message was from God himself. "Thus says the LORD . . ." punctuates their prophecies everywhere you look. If it's true that they were simply messengers charged with the duty of relaying God's warning – and the gracious offer of forgiveness if they repented – to his enemies, then we would do well to listen to them.

> And we have the word of the prophets made more certain, and you will do well to pay attention to it, as to a light shining in a dark place, until the day dawns and the morning star rises in your hearts. (2 Peter 1:19)

"More certain" means that the Lord's army is on the move, just as the prophets claimed. The signs are clear that the time is growing short and the opportunity to surrender before the "great and terrible day of the Lord" is slipping away. I know that many think that the world is just spinning around normally and life goes on from generation to generation the same as ever; but there will suddenly come a time when the Lord is going to stop everything and finish life as we know it – abruptly.

> They will say, "Where is this 'coming' he promised? Ever since our fathers died, everything goes on as it has since the beginning of creation." But they deliberately forget that long ago by God's Word the heavens existed and the earth was formed out of water and by water. By these waters also the world of that time was deluged and destroyed. By the same Word the present heavens and earth are reserved for fire, being kept for the day of judgment and destruction of ungodly men . . . But the day of the Lord will come like a thief. The heavens will disappear with a roar; the elements will be

destroyed by fire, and the earth and everything in it will be laid bare. (2 Peter 3:4-7,10)

The Prophets have *seen* this; they *know* the end is coming.

The problem here is that the Prophets are speaking of events from outside our world. Scientists tell us that the world runs by well-known physical principles – laws that Newton and Einstein taught us. And in such a well-ordered world, miracles simply cannot happen. That's why many modern people don't believe the Prophets of the Bible – they even accuse them of writing their prophecies *after* the event predicted and making it look as if they had written it *before* the event, so that we would think they were truly prophetic.

But there were millions of eyewitnesses in Bible times that will testify that miracles did happen, in spite of modern unbelief. God can and has come from Heaven to destroy the works of wickedness, upset earthly kingdoms, sweep away injustice and perversion – and set up a righteous kingdom in their place. We may doubt that such a thing can happen because *we* haven't seen it; but that doesn't mean it hasn't happened in the past and won't happen in the future, any more than doubting that George Washington ever existed will erase him from the history books.

The prophet, of course, suffered from the same problem that we have: unless God awakened his soul and gave life to his spiritual senses, he could no more know the mind of God than we can. He was as dead to the spiritual world of God as any other man. But God enabled the prophet to see spiritual realities, like the wrath of God and the army of God and the throne of the King of Heaven. He gave life to their souls and brought them, spiritually, into his presence in Heaven to witness what unaided mortal eyes could never see on their own. Isaiah describes it this way:

In the year that King Uzziah died, I saw the Lord seated on a throne, high and exalted, and the train of his robe filled the temple. Above him were seraphs, each with six wings: With two wings they covered their faces, with two they covered their feet, and with two they were flying. And they were calling to one another: "Holy, holy, holy is the LORD Almighty; the whole earth is full of his glory." At the sound of their voices the doorposts and thresholds shook and the temple was filled with smoke. "Woe to me!" I cried. "I am ruined! For I am a man of unclean lips, and I live among a people of unclean lips, and my eyes have seen the King, the LORD Almighty." (Isaiah 6:1-5)

In other words, the Spirit of God enabled him to see what the rest of us couldn't see. This is, in fact, one of the two major functions of the Holy Spirit – he reveals the reality of God to someone.

"No eye has seen, no ear has heard, no mind has conceived what God has prepared for those who love him" – but God has revealed it to us by his Spirit. The Spirit searches all things, even the deep things of God. For who among men knows the thoughts of a man except the man's spirit within him? In the same way no one knows the thoughts of God except the Spirit of God. We have not received the spirit of the world but the Spirit who is from God, that we may understand what God has freely given us. This is what we speak, not in words taught us by human wisdom but in words taught by the Spirit, expressing spiritual truths in spiritual words. (1 Corinthians 2:9-13)

The Spirit actually overcomes our physical limitations and enables us to know God; he reverses the curse of the Fall and reestablishes contact between God and man, as it was supposed to be from the original Creation.

So when God in his mercy decided to send messengers to the Israelites (and to us!) with the warning of his coming wrath and an offer of reconciliation, he first had to make the messenger *able* to see and understand the message. This is why any correct view of the Prophets in the Bible cannot accept the notion that they spoke on their own; they were no more able to know the mind and will of the invisible God than we are! The Spirit literally had to show them the whole picture and put the right words in their minds and hearts to repeat to us.

> Above all, you must understand that no prophecy of Scripture came about by the prophet's own interpretation. For prophecy never had its origin in the will of man, but men spoke from God as they were carried along by the Holy Spirit. (2 Peter 1:20-21)

People may not believe that, but that doesn't mean it's not true. Of course people will doubt the prophet – they haven't seen what the prophet saw! They don't have the Spirit enlightening them as the Prophet had. People have always doubted the Prophets.

> O Jerusalem, Jerusalem, you who kill the prophets and stone those sent to you, how often I have longed to gather your children together, as a hen gathers her chicks under her wings, but you were not willing. (Matthew 23:37)

Is there a proof that the message of the Prophets really is the Word of God? Yes, but it's not pretty, and it's certainly not to the liking of those who wait for it.

> You may say to yourselves, "How can we know when a message has not been spoken by the LORD?" If what a prophet proclaims in the name of the LORD does not take place or come true, that is a message the LORD has not spoken. That prophet has spoken presumptuously. Do not be afraid of him. (Deuteronomy 18:21-22)

And what did the prophet predict? The coming of the Lord and the destruction of the wicked! The only ones who will welcome the Lord's coming are those who *believed* the prophets' warning and offer, not doubted it. There will be no other "proof" of the Word of the Lord from the prophet except the prophecy coming true. This is why Jesus told the Pharisees –

> This is a wicked generation. It asks for a miraculous sign, but none will be given it except the sign of Jonah. For as Jonah was a sign to the Ninevites, so also will the Son of Man be to this generation. The Queen of the South will rise at the judgment with the men of this generation and condemn them; for she came from the ends of the earth to listen to Solomon's wisdom, and now one greater than Solomon is here. The men of Nineveh will stand up at the judgment with this generation and condemn it; for they repented at the preaching of Jonah, and now one greater than Jonah is here. (Luke 11:29-32)

The proof of a prophecy will be the drawn swords of the army of the Lord as they come with destruction in their wake, as the book of Revelation so graphically warns us. In times of war, the challenge is thrown down; the only proof that invading army will offer is blood and catastrophe.

> So be on your guard; I have told you everything ahead of time. But in those days, following that distress, 'the sun will be darkened, and the moon will not give its light; the stars will fall from the sky, and the heavenly bodies will be shaken.' At that time men will see the Son of Man coming in clouds with great power and glory. And he will send his angels and gather his elect from the four winds, from the ends of the earth to the ends of the heavens. (Mark 13:24-27)

This means that our only option is to *believe* the Prophets, while we still have the opportunity. The reward for faith is forgiveness and eternal life.

Witnesses

God is no fool. He knew that there would be determined resistance against his Bible, because first, people can't see the realities it talks of, and second, they don't like the message, being the sinners that they are. So he designed his Word in such a way that there simply isn't any way to escape the fact that it's the *truth*.

One brilliant method that he used was to employ eyewitnesses. An eyewitness is a person who was there at the event in question and personally saw it happen. We use the testimony of witnesses all the time in our culture to settle questions.

For example, let's enter a courtroom setting. The judge presides over a case in which a prosecuting attorney is bringing charges against the defendant. Arguments fly back and forth, reflecting different points of view, and the judge has to decide what the facts really are. Even physical evidence is brought to the table and argued over.

The judge has a critical role in the case because the life and well being of the defendant, as well as the integrity of the law, depend on him making a right judgment. So he needs all the facts possible, and discernment during the arguments, to make a right judgment.

There can be real doubt about a case when the two sides offer heated interpretations of what happened or didn't happen. But the doubt immediately clears up when one of the sides brings an eyewitness to the stand. He swears, under oath (and that's important), that he was there at the scene and saw exactly what happened. And since the eyewitness is sworn to tell the truth, the problem about what really happened is solved and the judge can make a right judgment. Not every case has an eyewitness available, nor are all eyewitnesses necessarily reliable; but the theory is sound. Our legal system depends heavily on the power of the witness to solve the case.

Now there are a few things about the eyewitness that we have to keep in mind:

- *First*, they are just as able as we are to discern what happened. They have the normal senses of a human being, and a mind to process the data. They can tell whether the accused stuck a knife in the victim or not. Even if the situation is more complicated than the average person could figure out, an "expert" witness who *does* know what was going on is sufficient (in the eyes of the Law) to decide the case.

- *Second*, they stand in our place. We weren't there at the scene, but they were. In the eyes of the court, it is not necessary for all of us to have been there in order to decide what really happened. The eyewitness represented us, so to speak, and can speak for all of us. What he saw and heard will do for all of us. Nobody can successfully argue with the judge that we can't accept their testimony just because someone we like better, or trust more, or even ourselves, weren't there at the scene. The court goes with the witness who was there.

- *Third,* because the testimony of an eyewitness is so powerful and conclusive, you must provide your own eyewitnesses to successfully challenge their testimony. It's not enough to say to the judge, "I don't like their testimony so I don't believe it." Calling an eyewitness a liar is a serious charge to make; the judge looks severely on perjury. So the court will demand that you provide conclusive proof in your challenge – which will entail finding your own witnesses who were there.

Now the greatest philosophical and religious question in history is this: is there a God, and what is he really like? Can we know the truth about God? Just as in a courtroom case, the debate has raged back and forth among all sorts of "experts" who have, unfortunately, come up with thousands of versions of who God is. One gets the feeling that nobody knows what they're talking about when they all contradict one another.

What we need is someone who has *seen* God and heard his voice. And that's exactly what we have in the Bible. It is actually a collection of affidavits of eyewitnesses who were there when he did his works on earth, and who heard his voice. And, as in the case of the courtroom, God carefully chose his witnesses to verify that he is what the Bible claims he is.

> He was **not** seen by all the people, but by **witnesses whom God had already chosen** – by us who ate and drank with him after he rose from the dead. He commanded us to preach to the people and to *testify* that he is the one whom God appointed as judge of the living and the dead. All the prophets *testify* about him that everyone who believes in him receives forgiveness of sins through his name. (Acts 10:41-43)

> We did not follow cleverly invented stories when we told you about the power and coming of

our Lord Jesus Christ, but we were *eyewitnesses* of his majesty. (2 Peter 1:16)

According to the Acts passage, not only were the Apostles eyewitnesses of Christ, but the prophets of the Old Testament "testified" about God, which means that they were witnesses too. You will find the theme of witnesses and testimony all through the Bible, from Genesis to Revelation. The reason that God deliberately chose this method of presenting his truth is so that *none of us have a good reason to reject it.*

What do the witnesses of the Bible testify to? Basically two kinds of things: *first*, the spiritual realities that man can't see on his own, and *second*, those uncomfortable realities that we don't like to think about.

- ***God himself*** – God is invisible; he lives in darkness and surrounds himself with mystery. (Psalm 97:2) In order to know whether there actually is a God, let alone what he's like, we need someone who has actually seen him. Philosophies and other types of guessing aren't good enough. So the Bible is full of testimonies from people who have seen God, heard his voice, and felt his hand upon them.
- ***Our sin*** – Due to our sin, we can't see how desperately wicked we are and the devastation that it has caused in our own lives and in the world around us. We are blind to the seriousness of sin, as you can tell by how little concern people have over it. But the witnesses of the Bible (primarily the Holy Spirit, through the ministry of the Prophets) uncover embarrassing hotbeds of immorality, rebellion, pride, greed, hatred, jealousy and murder in our hearts – and they also raise the alarm that

something must be done about this sin or we're going to die. They could see the doom of judgment hanging over our heads.

- ***Miracles*** – A miracle is something that God does himself, apart from any natural means. It's an event from outside the world; when the world needs help, God comes in and straightens out the problem that is, simply put, impossible for anybody else to do. From the Creation miracle all the way through to the miracles of Christ and the Apostles, we have ample testimony from eyewitnesses that God indeed uses miracles to do the impossible. If there is one lesson to learn from miracles it's the fact that we desperately need God's help!

- ***The coming Kingdom*** – As we mentioned under the subject of Prophets, the King is coming to destroy this world and set up a new Kingdom that's going to run according to righteousness and justice. The Prophets saw it coming. This world is flawed, empty, useless; God has no use for it besides a staging area to launch a new world where perfection will finally reign forever.

- ***Jesus Christ*** – There is probably nothing else in the Bible that requires so much, and gets so much, testimony as Jesus himself. The Father testified about him, the Prophets testified about him, the Apostles testified about him, and now the Church testifies about him. All their testimony focuses on several key points: that he really is the Son of God, that he really did come in the flesh, that he really does save any sinner who comes to him. Without this testimony, who would believe our report about him? (Isaiah

53:1) But what other fact in the Bible is so critical to believe for our eternal well being? Therefore God has sent overwhelming testimony to reveal the true nature of Christ and how we can take advantage of this offer of salvation in him.

- *The New Life* – Heaven is a goal of almost everyone, no matter what god or religion they hold to. But the Bible's witnesses testify of a particular place with certain characteristics. Sinners wouldn't like it there. Those who love the riches and glory of this world won't find any of that in Heaven. But those who long for freedom from sin, and who love the God that the Bible describes, will be glad to hear that Heaven is all that and much more that the reborn saint loves. Jesus came from Heaven to tell us what it's like there; Paul saw visions of it; the Prophets got word of it and reported on what they saw and heard; John also described it in detail.

- *Judgment Day* – It makes sense that there would be a Judgment Day, because God would naturally want to check his Creation to see if it performed according to his original commands. There were witnesses who got a glimpse and preview of that Day – and, according to them, it will be the terror of the wicked and the joy of the righteous. A lot of people are going to be surprised about what will and will not happen on Judgment Day. But they really don't have any excuse to be surprised, because God showed some of his people "what must soon take place" (Revelation 22:6) and we have their account in the Bible.

It doesn't make any sense to challenge the Bible accounts. For example, when God split the Red Sea, took his people across, and drowned Pharaoh's army, he had millions of eyewitnesses on hand to testify that it really did happen. Their testimony survives in the Exodus account. What if modern skeptics challenge that story and claim that it never took place? Well, that's not good enough. If you're going to call someone a liar, you must provide your own eyewitnesses who can testify that they were there and this thing never happened! If you can't produce any, the judge will tell you to shut up, sit down and quit disturbing the court with your opinions!

So far I have never found any modern skeptics who have provided eyewitnesses proving that the events in the Bible never happened.

Some people would object that if it were as easy as getting a witness to prove the Bible, then we would have to accept *any* religion that claims to have witnesses of their god. But you have to consider the unique case of the Bible. Other religions usually produce one or two or at most a handful of "witnesses" who supposedly saw their gods in action, and they passed on this information to their followers who simply adhere to the teaching of the original few. But as is typical with the true God, he does things in abundance. Instead of presenting a religion witnessed by one or two mystics, he brings in the testimony of millions of eyewitnesses over thousands of years. Millions of witnesses saw him split the Red Sea; thousands saw him kill the 185,000 enemy soldiers outside Jerusalem's walls in Hezekiah's day; thousands saw Jesus use a few loaves of fish to feed everyone there. As it says in Hebrews 12:1; "we are surrounded by such a great cloud of witnesses!"

Another thing to keep in mind is that God takes a dim view of lying witnesses.

There are six things the LORD hates, seven that are detestable to him . . . a false witness who pours out lies. (Proverbs 6:16,19)

A false witness will perish, and whoever listens to him will be destroyed forever. (Proverbs 21:28)

Someone's life hangs in the balance – ours, since the witness is supposedly testifying about how we can be saved from sin and death. If someone claims to have heard God and then spews out lies about sin and salvation, we who follow his testimony will die in our sins unsaved and our blood will be on his head. This again reminds us of the courtroom setting where the defendant's life hangs on the testimony of the eyewitness.

There is a primary witness to God, and there are secondary witnesses. What I'm referring to is the fact that man cannot know God or even see him without the help of the Holy Spirit. We looked at the fact that God has to reveal himself to us – we will never know the truth about him or the spiritual world unless he does. So even in the times when a person heard God's voice, or saw him in action in this world, what actually happened was that the Holy Spirit opened his eyes and ears to perceive the reality of God's presence.

An example of this principle is in the book of Kings when Elisha was being hunted by the king of Aram. His servant saw the enemy surrounding the city they were hiding in and was in a panic; how could the two of them survive when such an armed force was arrayed against them? But Elisha could see a bigger reality around them, and he prayed that the Lord would open the eyes of his servant so that he could see it too.

"Don't be afraid," the prophet answered. "Those who are with us are more than those who are with them." And Elisha prayed, "O LORD, open his eyes so he may see." Then the LORD opened the servant's eyes, and he looked and saw the hills full of horses and chariots of fire all around Elisha. (2 Kings 6:16-17)

There was no reason to fear the enemy when the Lord had an even stronger force arrayed against them!

We saw that the prophets saw God only because the Spirit enabled them to; they knew what to say to the Israelites because the Spirit gave them God's very words from his throne in Heaven. (2 Peter 1:20-21) In every instance when someone saw God, it was due to the influence of the Spirit of God – for example, when John saw a vision of Christ in his glory it was because John was "in the Spirit" that day. (Revelation 1:10) Even the false prophet Balaam spoke the words that Israel's God gave him because "the Spirit of God came upon him." (Numbers 24:2)

Jesus told Nicodemus that only those who were "born again" – meaning brought to life spiritually by the Holy Spirit – could see the Kingdom of God. (John 3:3,5) Jesus told his disciples that when the time came for them to go out to the nations and testify of him, he would fill them with the Holy Spirit (Acts 1:8) – a necessary qualification if they were going to get the story about him right!

The writer of Hebrews mentions, almost in an off-hand way, that the prophets of the Old Testament played no direct role in the creation of the Word of God. In the middle of discussing the sacrifice of Christ cleansing us from our sins, he states this:

> The Holy Spirit also testifies to us about this. First he says . . . (Hebrews 10:15)

And then he quotes Jeremiah 31. Note his comment – it wasn't Jeremiah who was speaking, but the Spirit of God!

The reason that it's important to establish the Holy Spirit as the primary witness behind all the testimony of human witnesses is this: he is the *Spirit of truth*. (John 14:17) He doesn't lie. And he isn't ignorant; he above all other witnesses is able to know God perfectly and get the facts straight about him. He will never tell us something that is inaccurate, or imperfect. If we go by what he says about the world of God, we can't go wrong. We may doubt human witnesses, but we have no reason to doubt the Spirit of God. In fact, it's just plain ignorance to doubt the one who made us.

That's why it's such a crime to accuse the Spirit of lying. When the Spirit testifies to us through the Word of God about what God is like, and even opens the eyes of human witnesses and provides the right words for their testimony of the same things, it's the height of ignorance and arrogance to claim that the whole thing is a myth! Anybody who does not believe the Bible – the testimony of the Spirit – is calling God a liar, if not a fool. And God doesn't take that lightly.

> Anyone who does not believe God has made him out to be a liar, because he has not believed the testimony God has given about his Son. (1 John 5:10)

> God is not a man, that he should lie, nor a son of man, that he should change his mind. (Numbers 23:19)

We are not overstating our case here. Remember that, in the courtroom, someone who doubts the eyewitness is actually accusing him of lying, and has to provide his own proof in the form of witnesses who can successfully challenge the perjury. *This is why God cast the Bible in the form of a collection of eyewitness accounts*. We cannot safely doubt the Bible. No one has successfully proven it wrong, at least in a way that would hold up in a court of law.

One further problem that we bring upon ourselves when we doubt the Bible is what we're going to experience on Judgment Day at the end of time. Because God used a *legal* device to present his case (that is, testimony), we are now obligated to accept it and go with it. If a judge declares the defendant innocent based on a witness' testimony, then no man has the right to treat that person as if he were guilty. In the eyes of the law, he is cleared of all guilt and everyone is obligated to treat him as such. In the same way, now that God has provided eyewitnesses to tell us the truth about him, we are now bound to accept that testimony *as truth* and act accordingly. We've been told about what God is like, and we've been told that we are sinners who are unacceptable to him. We've been told plainly the way to solve this problem – the simple steps of salvation in Christ. We have been told about the consequences of ignoring this salvation. We are now without excuse. This is why Jesus said,

> That servant who **knows** his master's will and does not get ready or does not do what his master wants will be beaten with many blows. (Luke 12:47)

As a crowning touch to his masterful argument, God is still providing eyewitnesses in our day. One of the Church's main purposes is to testify to the reality of God in this dark world.

> But you are a chosen people, a royal priesthood, a holy nation, a people belonging to God, that you may declare the praises of him who called you out of darkness into his wonderful light. Once you were not a people, but now you are the people of

God; once you had not received mercy, but now you have received mercy. (1 Peter 2:9-10)

We too know God now; we know that "he exists and that he rewards those who earnestly seek him." (Hebrews 11:6) As we hold out that light within us, and the world sees "Christ in us" (Colossians 1:27) and we tell others the reason for the "hope within us" (1 Peter 3:15), how can they doubt us without calling us liars? A testimony of what you have seen and heard is the most powerful tool you have to show others the reality of God.

God uses man

You've probably heard the old saying, "If you want something done right, do it yourself!" I have in my mind how I want things to look, so handing the project over to someone else may mean that it won't turn out the way I want it to.

In light of this, it's a wonder that God condescends to use man in such crucial works as the Bible, the Church, building the Kingdom of God, and other spiritual matters. Given the fact that man inevitably introduces imperfections and sins, and he simply doesn't have the perspective or mental scope that God brings to the project, why is he permitted to be part of the action? Wouldn't God have to continually follow along behind and restore what man has damaged?

Paul calls this "using the foolish for his purposes." Nobody can imagine a perfect God using imperfect man and coming up with anything we can take seriously – let alone stake our eternal souls on! Yet in God's profound wisdom, that's exactly what he does.

> For Christ did not send me to baptize, but to preach the gospel – not with words of human wisdom, lest the cross of Christ be emptied of its power. For the message of the cross is foolishness to those who are perishing, but to us who are being saved it is the power of God. For it is written: "I will destroy the wisdom of the wise; the intelligence of the intelligent I will frustrate."

> Where is the wise man? Where is the scholar? Where is the philosopher of this age? Has not God made foolish the wisdom of the world? For since in the wisdom of God the world through its wisdom did not know him, God was pleased through the foolishness of what was preached to save those who believe.
>
> Jews demand miraculous signs and Greeks look for wisdom, but we preach Christ crucified: a stumbling block to Jews and foolishness to Gentiles, but to those whom God has called, both Jews and Greeks, Christ the power of God and the wisdom of God. For the foolishness of God is wiser than man's wisdom, and the weakness of God is stronger than man's strength.
>
> Brothers, think of what you were when you were called. Not many of you were wise by human standards; not many were influential; not many were of noble birth. But God chose the foolish things of the world to shame the wise; God chose the weak things of the world to shame the strong. He chose the lowly things of this world and the despised things – and the things that are not – to nullify the things that are, so that no one may boast before him. (1 Corinthians 1:17-29)

In this passage is the heart of how God does his spiritual works in this world. He insists on using fallible people to do his work on earth – for a reason: he wants all the glory. In other words, when we can clearly see that the people he uses are poor, ignorant nobodies, who then is responsible when the thing actually works? It's obvious that God overruled the problems and got the job done anyway.

And yet the work that he does is nothing less than God at work, not man. The words that the Prophets spoke were God's words; the miracles that Moses and Paul did were from the hand of God. Somehow through the human we meet the Divine.

God does not come to earth in person, in his full spiritual glory, to do his work. The experience would unmake us. Whenever he "touches down" on earth, so to speak, the mountains themselves quake and the seas roar.

> He rebukes the sea and dries it up; he makes all the rivers run dry. Bashan and Carmel wither and the blossoms of Lebanon fade. The mountains quake before him and the hills melt away. The earth trembles at his presence, the world and all who live in it. (Nahum 1:4-5)

To minimize the impact on earth, to water it down enough that we can handle it without dying in the encounter ("You cannot see my face, for no one may see me and live" – Exodus 33:20), he uses created things – including man – to do his work here. This means, however, that he has to accommodate himself to our limitations – including our sins, ignorance, willfulness, physical needs and ailments.

The wonder is that God can work in the middle of all these problems of ours and still accomplish his goals! This is where the doctrine of miracles comes into play. He can raise the dead; he can open the eyes of the blind; he can calm the storm; he can split the sea in two. He can also speak his Word to a mortal man (enabling him to see spiritual realities), preserve that Word intact through the ages, and aim it at my heart two thousand years later through the one who preaches (and who doesn't even know that *my* heart is the intended target!) to change me forever. God isn't worried in the least about the "imperfections" of the Bible. He created the whole system – and he includes sinful and imperfect works of man in the process – so that it *works*.

God never did expect man to be able to build a spiritual kingdom. Our problem is that we have only five senses, enough to manipulate the physical world around us but no more. We understand how to carve and erect stone for a church, we know how to make paper and ink for books, we know how to make public address systems and media so that thousands can hear a speaker. And God mysteriously works through these physical means to change a heart from sin to holiness.

The power comes from behind, within, and through the works of man. God takes what we all know can't work and transforms it into an irresistible force. Remember when Jesus took the five loaves of bread from the young boy and blessed them? He then used them to feed 5000 men plus the women and children present. The impossible happened. He was showing the disciples how to go out in their own ministries and do likewise. Through them – some of them unlettered fishermen, none of them religious experts – God would build an eternal Church.

There are problems in the Bible, there's no denying it. For example, many people argue about which version of the Bible to use. Did you know that this argument isn't just over personal preferences? The real problem is that those versions are based on different Bible texts! Over the centuries there were manuscript "families" that accumulated in certain geographic areas – manuscripts that shared the same wording and even errors. The translators, therefore, had to pick which Greek and Hebrew texts to work from, which leads to many of the variations that we have in our versions today.

Another problem is that the Bible didn't just drop out of Heaven one day, ready-made, in its present form. It came about over thousands of years, in pieces here and there, and went through many hands in the process. In other words, the Bible grew and developed over a long time. The books were written in response to individual needs and circumstances, in cultures strange to us, originally for their use, not ours! What are we to think about a book that developed in this way?

However, the most serious problem about the Bible is this: we do not have the original Bible. Whatever scrolls or parchments the Biblical authors wrote their books on were lost long ago. The Bibles that we have today are based on copies of copies of copies, and nobody really knows how much or how little those copies deviated from the original written books. Out of the thousands of manuscripts of the Bible that exist today, there are many deviations and variations in the text that have caused scholars and translators centuries of labor trying to decide what the original actually read like.

Many people, when they hear about these kinds of things, decide not to believe the Bible anymore. Why should they depend on a book with mistakes in it? How can anybody believe that the Bible is the Word of God when it is so obviously a work of man?

But we have to learn to distinguish between man's works and God's works, and put our trust in what God does regardless of what man does. Let's start with the premise that the Bible is the Word of God (based on what we've seen so far). Is there a way to account for the problems? Of course – when the Bible was first written, each author put down the words that God had put in his head and heart. *The original copy was direct from Heaven.* In theology they call the original copies the **autographs** – the actual documents that Moses and Isaiah and the Apostle John and the rest actually wrote down first.

From that point on, man began showing his weakness and imperfections in the way he transmitted the text from generation to generation. In fact, for over 3000 years the Bible has been copied, translated, and distributed around the world with varying degrees of care. Unfortunately none of the autographs survived. And that's our major problem right now – nobody knows exactly how the autographs read, or how far off our present copies are from those originals.

In our modern era (at least since the Reformation) the Church has been greatly interested in how well the Bible has held up over the centuries. The search for earlier and more ancient manuscripts has been intense. The idea is that if we can find copies of the Bible that were made not long after the autographs themselves, they would (theoretically!) have less copying errors than later manuscripts. The search has been highly successful and has turned up surprising results. For example, they have Greek manuscripts of the New Testament that date only a couple of hundred years after the autographs. And the differences between those early copies and later ones consist of trivial details – the word "and" is in this copy and not in the other one, for example.

What this means is that people have taken great care to copy and translate the Bible as accurately as possible, and it's obvious that their care has paid off. Compared to other ancient books, our present editions of the Bible are accurate and faithful to the original.

It's easy to criticize the Bible for its inaccuracies and problems, but it's not honest to ignore the fact that the doctrines of the Bible are the same no matter what translation or manuscript you're looking at. For example, here is John 3:3 in several translations:

I tell you the truth, no one can see the kingdom of God unless he is born again. (NIV)

Verily, verily, I say unto thee, Except a man be born again, he cannot see the kingdom of God. (KJV)

Truly, I say to you, Without a new birth no man is able to see the kingdom of God. (BEV)

Amen, amen, I say to thee, unless a man be born again, he cannot see the kingdom of God. (DRV)

Truly, truly, I say to you, unless one is born again, he cannot see the kingdom of God. (NASV)

In all truth I tell you, no one can see the kingdom of God without being born from above. (NJB)

Truly, truly, I say to you, unless one is born anew, he cannot see the kingdom of God. (RSV)

Verily, verily, I say to thee, If any one may not be born from above, he is not able to see the reign of God. (YLT)

All these versions come from the following Greek verse:

ἀμὴν ἀμὴν λέγω σοι, ἐὰν μή τις γεννηθῇ ἄνωθεν,
οὐ δύναται ἰδεῖν τὴν βασιλείαν τοῦ θεοῦ.

No matter what the translation, there's no getting around the fact of what Jesus is saying: to see and know the spiritual world of God, we have to be "born again" or "born from above" (the Greek word allows either translation). One wonders why people stumble over textual differences between manuscripts (that don't affect basic Christian doctrine anyway), and show absolutely no concern about the state of their souls described in plain texts like this one. They argue about trivia and use that to discredit the salvation message in the Bible.

People who turn away from the Bible because it has "imperfections" are deliberately ignoring the plain and simple truths that the Bible teaches in every language. They are "straining out gnats" (as Jesus said) to avoid the Bible's teaching, while "swallowing camels" of deceit from pagan religions and philosophies. (Matthew 23:24)

There's a reason for this, of course – they don't want to look the true God square in the face. They don't want to hear the truth. Sinners don't want to leave their sin; they'd rather wallow in rebellion and perversion than surrender to God and become holy. So in an effort to belittle the Bible and its penetrating message, they find fault with it. In logic we call this argument "argumentum ad hominem" – an attack against the *person*, instead of facing the *point* itself. That's not an acceptable argument – it is, in fact, well known as a logical fallacy. It certainly doesn't make the Bible go away!

The power of the Bible is plain when, in spite of the problems and weaknesses, it grips the heart with eternal issues. Through the Bible, God has brought terrible fear on men's hearts, he has lifted them up in spiritual ecstasy, he has cleared the fog around their situation and made the path to life very plain, he has encouraged those who despair, he has brought back the sinner from his filth, he has instilled undying love for God and man in the hardest hearts. Millions of people can testify to the power of God's Word. Ask them where all these life-changing feelings and emotions have come from and they will point to the Bible – through something they read there, God has touched and changed their hearts. There is simply no denying the testimony of all these witnesses.

Anybody who can resurrect a dead body from the grave and completely restore him to life can certainly overcome all problems and shortcomings that man might bring to the situation! God's arm is not so short that he is stumped with problems and impossibilities. *We* may not be able to understand how he can take the frailties and ignorance of men and use it to save souls, but that's no limitation for the Creator. He can use even those who most hate him to accomplish his purposes.

> The LORD works out everything for his own ends – even the wicked for a day of disaster. (Proverbs 16:4)

I doubt that we will ever solve the manuscript problem of the Bible, just as I doubt that there will ever be a perfect preacher, or Christian, or Church – not in this world. There will always be, in God's wisdom, a "stone that makes men stumble" (1 Peter 2:8) "Wise" men will continue to find holes and problems in the Bible and the Church; the "great" in this world's eyes will continue to despise and discount the works of God that seem to struggle on through so many problems and limitations.

But Judgment Day will be an eye-opener. The very thing that the "wise" despised will turn out to be our salvation. The Bible really is the truth, God really is what the Word says he is, Jesus really is our only Savior, and the wicked and unbelieving really are going to suffer in eternal torment. It will turn out that the truth was right under our noses the whole time; it would have been as simple as picking up the Word, reading it, and believing it. It's too simple, it seems, for the "wise" and powerful to do, so they will be lost. Only the "children" will be rewarded for their faith.

> I praise you, Father, Lord of Heaven and earth, because you have hidden these things from the wise and learned, and revealed them to little children. Yes, Father, for this was your good pleasure. (Matthew 11:25-26)

But it's not only Judgment Day that will separate the sheep from the goats. Because people refuse to go to the Bible for life, they suffer *now* under the thorns and trials of life – needlessly!

> But the way of the wicked is like deep darkness; they do not know what makes them stumble. (Proverbs 4:19)

God's people, however, in spite of the problems of life, feast at the table of God in the Word and experience peace, joy, forgiveness, love, power – all the fruits of Heaven.

> The path of the righteous is like the first gleam of dawn, shining ever brighter till the full light of day. (Proverbs 4:18)

> Your Word is a lamp to my feet and a light for my path. (Psalm 119:105)

A Book for Faith

Faith is a gift from God. Contrary to popular opinion, one can't decide to believe in God, or hold to certain doctrines of God, and expect this to pass for faith. We have to keep in mind that an unaided human being is incapable of knowing the true God or even wanting to. If such a thing is to happen, God himself has to step in and give us a spiritual ability that we don't naturally possess.

> . . . in accordance with the measure of faith God has *given* you. (Romans 12:3)

> For it is by grace you have been saved, through faith – and this not from yourselves, it is the *gift* of God – not by works, so that no one can boast. (Ephesians 2:8)

Faith, the book of Hebrews tells us, is "being sure of what we hope for and certain of what we do not see." (Hebrews 11:1) The Bible is trying to show us a spiritual God, and the spiritual world that he lives in; but our physical senses can't grasp such realities. So the Lord awakens our spirits within us; he turns on our spiritual senses. Now we can see God! Now when he speaks to us, we can hear him. We know God is real just as much as we know the chair we're sitting in is real. So the world we can't see suddenly becomes so real that we are "sure" and "certain" of it.

The writer of Hebrews goes on to give us examples of people who were awakened and saw the world of God.

> And without faith it is impossible to please God, because anyone who comes to him **must believe that he exists** and that he rewards those who earnestly seek him. (Hebrews 11:6)

> By faith Moses, when he had grown up, refused to be known as the son of Pharaoh's daughter. He chose to be mistreated along with the people of God rather than to enjoy the pleasures of sin for a short time. He regarded disgrace for the sake of Christ as of greater value than the treasures of Egypt, because he was looking ahead to his reward. By faith he left Egypt, not fearing the king's anger; he persevered because **he saw him who is invisible**. (Hebrews 11:24-27)

Faith penetrates the fog of this world to God's world beyond and behind the physical universe. Usually in order to see the truth, we have to literally ignore the problems that loom up in the way. For example, we've seen that the Bible is a problematic book because man was involved in its making. So *in spite of* different translations, *in spite of* manuscript errors and differences – through faith we are able to see the Bible as the Word of God.

> And we also thank God continually because, when you received the Word of God, which you heard from us, you accepted it not as the word of men, but as it actually is, the Word of God, which is at work in you who believe. (1 Thessalonians 2:13)

Certainly wherever man is involved in something there will be problems. But the part that God provides is infallible and pure. Man's involvement (no matter how imperfect) doesn't blunt the sharp edge of God's truth if he wants to impale someone's heart with it! (After all, he once used a donkey to rebuke a man!) Once we see that, the problems fade into the background as unimportant. Someone without faith gets stopped at the outer door, so to speak, and can't get past the problems.

People had the same problem with Jesus himself. The Pharisees saw a troublemaker in him; the crowds, a miracle-worker and wise teacher; his townsfolk, the son of Joseph the carpenter. But to a select few he was the Son of God.

> "But what about you?" he asked. "Who do you say I am?" Simon Peter answered, "You are the Christ, the Son of the living God." Jesus replied, "Blessed are you, Simon son of Jonah, *for this was not revealed to you by man, but by my Father in Heaven*." (Matthew 16:15-17)

The goal of faith is that we might see God in his Word, that we might hear his voice in the Bible as he speaks to us. We need to make this contact with God – our souls are at stake. He is going to probe our hearts and root out the sin and rebellion there that is killing us. He's going to send his Spirit to fill our hearts with the grace of Christ himself, the Light and Life of Heaven, so that we can live in the presence of God. He's going to prepare us for living with him in Heaven – something that flesh and blood can't do, but a resurrected body and soul can. We're going to need wisdom, lots of it, to cooperate with God in this venture – he doesn't want us to back away in fear or apathy, or to make things difficult for him. This is why Paul prayed that we might have more faith to see God more clearly; much is at stake here.

> I keep asking that the God of our Lord Jesus Christ, the glorious Father, may give you the Spirit of wisdom and revelation, so that you may know him better. I pray also that the eyes of your heart may be enlightened in order that you may know the hope to which he has called you, the riches of his glorious inheritance in the saints, and his

incomparably great power for us who believe. (Ephesians 1:17-19)

One of the most important areas we have to work on is our sin. It takes a lot of thought and soul-searching, and a willingness to "submit to the Father of our spirits and live." (Hebrews 12:9) We have to be willing to come to him in his Word, surrender, hold out helpless hands like a child, and plead for his mercy. We need Christ to bring us to the Father for reconciliation. We need the Spirit to cleanse our hearts and minds from impurity. Reading the Bible requires a humble attitude. God's standards of holiness are so high, and we fall so short of the goal, that it will take a lifetime of humility and reproof and correction to get us ready for Heaven. (2 Timothy 3:16)

But we will do none of this if we don't see the awe-inspiring holiness of God and the precious value of the salvation he has put in Christ for those who will come.

> You diligently study the Scriptures because you think that by them you possess eternal life. These are the Scriptures that testify about me, yet you refuse to come to me to have life. (John 5:39-40)

There are those who think that "faith" is just another word for being gullible. In the name of "faith" the masses are asked to believe whatever the Church wants them to believe, with no more proof than "if it's meant to be, you'll see it; if not, too bad."

But that charge can be made against many other things that we're asked to believe in! Is there anybody still living who witnessed the Revolutionary War? Yet nobody in their right mind would doubt it, because there are so many evidences and testimonies left from that time period that convince us it really happened. One *could* doubt it, I suppose, but a reasonable person has to draw the line somewhere and admit that the evidence for it is overwhelming and not open to doubt.

We've already looked at the fact that the Bible has more eyewitness testimony than any other ancient document in history. And people in our own day testify that the message is still the same, and the same spiritual results occur when one believes. One *could* doubt it, but it would entail calling millions upon millions of people liars and fools, if not criminal. It would be more reasonable to assume that someone who doesn't see the preciousness of the Bible does not yet have the spiritual skill to penetrate its mystery.

A sobering aspect of this matter of faith is that God many times denies people the ability to see the truth. He will actually cloud their minds so that they can't see the truth in the Word. The prophets describe this:

> Go and tell this people: 'Be ever hearing, but never understanding; be ever seeing, but never perceiving.' Make the heart of this people calloused; make their ears dull and close their eyes. Otherwise they might see with their eyes, hear with their ears, understand with their hearts, and turn and be healed. (Isaiah 6:9-10)

Jesus deliberately spoke in parables to hide the meaning of his lessons from the majority of the crowd. It seems as if he was punishing them in this way – they once had the chance to hear and believe the truth, but since they turned their backs on God's Word, he's certainly not going to let them have a second chance to reject him!

> The disciples came to him and asked, "Why do you speak to the people in parables?" He replied, "The knowledge of the secrets of the kingdom of

> Heaven has been given to you, but not to them. Whoever has will be given more, and he will have an abundance. Whoever does not have, even what he has will be taken from him. This is why I speak to them in parables: 'Though seeing, they do not see; though hearing, they do not hear or understand.'" (Matthew 13:10-13)

God is King. This well-known idea has some chilling consequences to it. If the King decides that you are no longer worthy of his treasures that you seem to despise, he will withdraw from you any further access to it.

> Therefore consider carefully how you listen. Whoever has will be given more; whoever does not have, even what he thinks he has will be taken from him. (Luke 8:18)

In other words, this person will no longer be able to understand the Bible; it will be nonsense to him, he will distort it to his own perverted desires, it will prove to be a curse to him in the end because he will turn to a perverted life of wickedness that the Bible condemns. If a person wants to live in the gutter, God certainly isn't going to give him his treasures to make filthy.

> Do not give dogs what is sacred; do not throw your pearls to pigs. If you do, they may trample them under their feet, and then turn and tear you to pieces. (Matthew 7:6)

What we're saying here is that it's a fearful thing not to understand and appreciate the Bible. Such a state of mind could very well be a curse. And it would not be a good idea to aggravate the situation by calling God a liar and the Bible a farce!

This surely accounts for our present society's ignorance and contempt of the Bible. From the eighteenth century on, the Western world has found more and more reasons to discount the stories of the Bible and to change the rules of morality that are so plainly written there. As things stand now, very few people believe the Bible anymore; they've been talked out of it by atheistic science and psychology and philosophy. Most schools – especially Bible colleges and seminaries which train pastors and Bible teachers – include some sort of training which explains away some or most of the Bible's teaching.

> For the time will come when men will not put up with sound doctrine. Instead, to suit their own desires, they will gather around them a great number of teachers to say what their itching ears want to hear. They will turn their ears away from the truth and turn aside to myths. (2 Timothy 4:3)

But let's get the order straight. When people turn away from the Word of God – the declarations from the Throne of Heaven that have authority over our lives – then God just may turn away from them and make it impossible for them to know him and be saved. This is "reprobation" – taking away the possibility of salvation. He certainly did it to Israel!

> What then? What Israel sought so earnestly it did not obtain, but the elect did. The others were hardened, as it is written: "God gave them a spirit of stupor, eyes so that they could not see and ears so that they could not hear, to this very day." And David says: "May their table become a snare and a trap, a stumbling block and a retribution for them. May their eyes be darkened so they cannot see, and their backs be bent forever." (Romans 11:7-10)

When people don't see the point of the Bible, will God hold them accountable? Oh, yes – they will be held guilty for what they already know about God (which is enough to condemn them – see Paul's argument in Romans 1-3), even if they don't understand the additional information in the Bible. *All* people are sinners because *all* have turned away from the Creator; their consciences will testify against them on Judgment Day that this is so. What is tragic is that God may shut them out from the Tree of Life (Genesis 3:24) – the Word of God – so that they cannot know the way to be saved from their sin.

So, what should our response be? First, it's obvious that we can't turn the light on ourselves. Faith doesn't come through one's own efforts. If you want this treasure from God, you have to come to him on his terms, not yours. No demanding proofs, no insisting on miracles, just repent, surrender and wait on his will. Not only is the question of your eternal state in his hands, but even the means of doing anything about it is *his* to give.

> "All things have been committed to me by my Father. No one knows who the Son is except the Father, and no one knows who the Father is except the Son and those to whom the Son chooses to reveal him." Then he turned to his disciples and said privately, "Blessed are the eyes that see what you see. For I tell you that many prophets and kings wanted to see what you see but did not see it, and to hear what you hear but did not hear it." (Luke 10:22-24)

So the apostle James recommends that we come to God asking for wisdom and insight – you certainly can't get it on your own. But the person who honors God by believing that the Bible is truly the Word of God will get everything he asks for. God loves prayers like that! What he hates is any trace of a doubt that the things of God, as described carefully and clearly in the Bible, are true.

> If any of you lacks wisdom, he should ask God, who gives generously to all without finding fault, and it will be given to him. But when he asks, he must believe and not doubt, because he who doubts is like a wave of the sea, blown and tossed by the wind. That man should not think he will receive anything from the Lord; he is a double-minded man, unstable in all he does. (James 1:5-8)

Unbelief

> Blind unbelief is sure to err,
>   and scan his works in vain;
> God is his own interpreter,
>   and he will make it plain.
> *William Cowper, 1774*

Cowper put his finger on the problem with unbelief – if someone doesn't believe the truth, then he will believe a lie. And our great enemy the devil, who would love to steer us away from the truth, is doing everything he can to get people to believe lies about God's Word.

> Why is my language not clear to you? Because you are unable to hear what I say. You belong to your father, the devil, and you want to carry out your father's desire. He was a murderer from the beginning, not holding to the truth, for there is no truth in him. When he lies, he speaks his native language, for he is a liar and the father of lies. (John 8:43-44)

For the last two hundred years at least, there's been a determined attack against the Bible. Modern man has discovered, through science in particular, a new freedom and power over his world that the ancients never enjoyed. So why fear the "gods" of the world when you can run the world yourself? And the Bible is a thorn in their side, because it represents the "old" standard that "naïve" people of the past believed. It certainly doesn't allow a free lifestyle that our modern world makes so easy. So to remove the thorn, "experts" have been busy destroying the foundations of the Bible so that now only "ignorant" people would take it at face value.

Liberalism (which is the formal name for the wave of unbelief that has swept the Western world in the last two centuries) is a way, or method, of looking at the Bible – basically, it doesn't believe it. Liberals want to keep the name Christian, but they don't want the doctrine of Christianity. It's amazing what they don't believe! They have more in common with pagan religions than the faith that the Apostles once taught.

Liberals don't believe in –

- ***Miracles*** – They don't believe in anything supernatural – the miracles of Christ, the miracles that Moses did in the wilderness (starting with the plagues in Egypt and the parting of the Red Sea), the miracles that the Apostles did, the miracles that the Prophets did. They especially don't believe in the very first miracle in the Bible, the biggest one of them all – the Creation!

- ***Blood atonement*** – The Liberals don't believe that the blood of any person or of any animal can cleanse our hearts of sin. Since the Old Testament sacrificial system depended on the blood sacrifice of animals to reconcile God and man, they claim that the whole bloody system was a carry-over from pagan religions. They are particularly offended at the thought that Jesus' death was demanded by God, and that it would bring God and man together in reconciliation, and that his blood was necessary to "cover over" (which is what the word "atonement" means in Hebrew) our sinful hearts. And of course the reason they don't believe in blood atonement is because they don't believe that man has done anything serious enough to warrant someone's death as punishment.

- *Prophecy* – Since Liberals don't believe in the supernatural, they can't believe that the prophets actually predicted events before they happened. So by their account, the Prophets wrote their "predictions" after the events happened (which explains why they were so accurate!) and then claimed to have written them before the events – sort of a pious fraud for the benefit of God's people.

- *Original authorship* – The Liberals don't believe that Moses wrote the first five books of Moses, they don't believe that Isaiah wrote Isaiah, they don't believe that Daniel wrote Daniel, (that is, they claim that the prophecies that Daniel supposedly uttered were put into his mouth by editors centuries later), they don't believe that Matthew wrote Matthew, they don't believe that Paul wrote most of the letters ascribed to him, and they have problems with many of the other books in the Bible. The reason is that they don't want to give *any credence at all* to what the Bible says about itself, not even to who actually wrote the books.

- *The integrity of the Gospels* – For over three hundred years the Liberals have been trying to destroy the story of Jesus. Their claim is that the Church, or the Apostles, turned the simple morality teachings of Jesus the Jew into a new religion that made him God. Supposedly the Gospel accounts are actually fictitious myths of the early Church; we can't really know what Jesus was really like.

- ***The integrity of the original manuscripts*** – There are whole sciences devoted to the study of the original documents of the Bible (they are known as "form criticism" and "textual criticism"), and their goal is to show how undependable the Bible is. Not only do they "prove" that the Bibles we have now are simply corrupted and unreliable copies of whatever the originals may have been (since nobody can know what they were like!), they also demonstrate that the Israelites and the Church borrowed very heavily from their cultures to form the Bible. In other words, just as we would use a saying from Shakespeare to make a point in our sermons, the Biblical writers used common themes and ideas in their day to form their new religion. So, the Liberals tell us, it was *not* revelation from another world. The pagan world already had these ideas worked out, and the Bible writers collected them together to form both Judaism and Christianity. Sort of like a religious plagiarism.

- ***The Bible as the Word of God*** – With all these problems, the Liberals have come to the conclusion that the Bible can't be the Word of God. It's obviously a work of man, full of problems, contradictions and myths. The Old Testament in particular is an immature religious work of the Jews; interesting, but not very helpful for modern man except for some morality lessons. The New Testament contains outright falsehoods from a Church anxious to lift their new "God" to divine status among the world's pantheon of gods. Just the embarrassing situation of thousands of manuscripts rarely agreeing about how the text reads should prove to anybody that the Bible is not a perfect work from Heaven!

Why would the Liberals bother to study the Bible, then, if they don't believe most of it? *First*, it gives them the aura of authority they need for their own agenda. They can claim to be teaching the Bible, get unsuspecting students to sit at their feet, and then give them everything *but* the Bible. These Bible "scholars" spend more time destroying people's faith in the Bible than they do teaching its precepts, yet they are held in high esteem by the Church and society. They genuinely think that they are doing a service to God! (See John 16:2) Their degrees and positions in Christian circles open many doors for them; they dominate educational institutions; they dictate and direct the agenda of the Church in modern society. But they are impostors, wolves in sheep's clothing.

> For certain men whose condemnation was written about long ago have secretly slipped in among you. They are godless men, who change the grace of our God into a license for immorality and deny Jesus Christ our only Sovereign and Lord . . . In the very same way, these dreamers pollute their own bodies, reject authority and slander celestial beings. Yet these men speak abusively against whatever they do not understand; and what things they do understand by instinct, like unreasoning animals – these are the very things that destroy them . . . Woe to them! They have taken the way of Cain; they have rushed for profit into Balaam's error; they have been destroyed in Korah's rebellion. These men are blemishes at your love feasts, eating with you without the slightest qualm – shepherds who feed only themselves. They are clouds without rain, blown along by the wind; autumn trees, without fruit and uprooted – twice dead. They are wild waves of the sea, foaming up their shame; wandering stars, for whom blackest darkness has been reserved forever. (Jude 4,8,10-13)

Second, it pays the bills. There's a lot of money to be made in the service of the Church. Would people actually be dishonest and use the Bible and the Church as a vehicle to material gain? Absolutely! If they jumped to another religion they wouldn't have the opportunities they have under the Church's umbrella. Life is good if you can stay in the Church, come up with your own doctrines, enjoy the fruits of immorality, and get paid for it too! Paul knew about these kinds of parasites in the Church.

> If anyone teaches false doctrines and does not agree to the sound instruction of our Lord Jesus Christ and to godly teaching, he is conceited and understands nothing. He has an unhealthy interest in controversies and quarrels about words that result in envy, strife, malicious talk, evil suspicions and constant friction between men of corrupt mind, who have been robbed of the truth and who think that godliness is a means to financial gain. (1 Timothy 6:3-5)

The Liberal agenda is actually to create a new God for people to believe in, and they have given us a chopped-up Bible that includes only a few pious devotions that they are comfortable promoting. This God of theirs will allow them to do what the ancients called sin and wickedness:

> Do you not know that the wicked will not inherit the kingdom of God? Do not be deceived: Neither the sexually immoral nor idolaters nor adulterers nor male prostitutes nor homosexual offenders nor thieves nor the greedy nor drunkards nor slanderers nor swindlers will inherit the kingdom of God. (1 Corinthians 6:9-10)

That list pretty much describes what many of our modern churches (and the government has followed their lead and legalized a lot of it) allow and even promote. They are after state-sponsored, church-sanctioned immorality. So the goal is to thoroughly discredit the Bible as revelation from God.

> Where there is no revelation, the people cast off restraint; but blessed is he who keeps the law. (Proverbs 29:18)

Liberal theology actually gives a great deal of relief to someone looking for a way out of the strict requirements of the Kingdom of God. If they can show that the Bible is a work of man, and basically undependable (to some degree or another – not all of them draw the lines in the same places), then its opinions aren't any better than yours or mine. If they can prove that the Bible is contradictory and imperfect, then that means we don't have to take it so seriously. What God said about right and wrong in Moses' day just may be a cultural thing and totally inappropriate for our day. If they can easily explain away the integrity and authority of the Bible (even for such a simple thing as who wrote the books!), then we are free to question everything in it – especially the parts where God makes uncomfortable demands on us! And isn't that the case? Even those people who say they believe the Bible end up contradicting each other with different views, so that everyone is confused and the Bible doesn't seem to be a real help for anybody – so obviously (the unbelievers tell us) people are taking an imperfect book way too seriously.

In the days of the early Church, such rank unbelievers would be shown to the door – and branded as heretics so that others in the community would know to stay away from them. In our day that's considered impolite behavior, so we let them stay and corrupt the minds of our youth with their poison. Now it's rare to find a church, and almost impossible to find a school, that hasn't been infected to some degree or another with Liberalism.

As to the things they deny, we've already looked at many things about the Bible that would challenge their claims. Let's look now at the fundamental problems of Liberalism, or unbelief in general.

First, they weren't there. So how can they arrogantly declare that the events in the Bible didn't happen as described there? How can a person in the twenty-first century claim that a man in Jesus' day lied in his account of the resurrection of Lazarus? John was there; the modern critic was not. No amount of theory can dismiss an eyewitness account. Such a foolish argument would be immediately shut down in a court of law as inadmissible.[2] If unbelievers want me to accept their watered-down version of the stories in the Bible, they're going to have to come up with reliable witnesses of their own who can show me, without any doubt, that the Bible writers were **lying**.

Second, their agenda is unacceptable. Unbelievers want to be free of the moral restraints of the Bible – that's why they're trying to destroy its authority. They want to be free to live immoral lives with a clear conscience. Of course they don't say that in their books, or in public; but watch them in everyday life and you will see that this is what they are after. It's sin that they love, and the Bible condemns sinners.[3] So, out with the Bible!

Third, they are being completely dishonest. If they really want to throw out most of the Bible, the least they could do is

---

[2] In the early nineteenth century Simon Greenleaf, a professor of Law, co-creator of Harvard's law program, and trial lawyer himself, wrote an analysis of the Gospels in light of a court case. He found that the Gospels were so well presented that no critic could bring a successful case against them. ***The Testimony of the Evangelists***, Simon Greenleaf; Kregel: Grand Rapids.

[3] In a private letter, Thomas Huxley ("Darwin's bulldog") admitted that one of the reasons he fought so hard for the theory of evolution is so that people would have the freedom to indulge in sexual immorality. A perfect fulfillment of Ephesians 4:18-19!

drop the name "Christian" and form some new pagan religion. They're causing a great deal of confusion in the Church by hiding under the Church's umbrella of protection and financial security. Young people in particular are susceptible to authority, and they usually don't have the discernment they need to spot a clever liar and cheat. Yet they're being indoctrinated with the Liberal's brand of "Christianity" and losing their souls in the process. Jesus' condemnation of the Pharisees leading new converts into their wickedness comes to mind here. (Matthew 23:15)

Fourth, it doesn't work. As much as the Liberals fight against the Bible and try to talk people out of it, the Spirit of God overrules and convinces the child of God that it really is the Word of God. Fortunately God is bigger than man is, and when he wants someone to believe the truth, no amount of lies and strategy is going to prevail against the Spirit of Truth. Most people will fall for the lie; but the children know bread when they see it!

> When the Gentiles heard this, they were glad and honored the Word of the Lord; and all who were appointed for eternal life believed. (Acts 13:48)

So unbelief is neither honest nor wise. There's too much about the Bible to casually dismiss; you need to provide legitimate evidence and testimony to successfully denounce it – certainly not mere opinions! Besides, the reason people want to belittle the Bible is to get more freedom to live in sin and ignore God's plain directives for life, though they're not honest enough to admit it.

Unbelievers often are the ones demanding "proof" for the things of God. The Pharisees in Jesus' day were the ones who caused problems in his ministry; they had no intention of believing anything he said – they just wanted a pretext for getting rid of him. But God will not cater to unbelief; he doesn't owe unbelievers a thing! He is the King, and he demands *obedience*. He is not pleased with a rebellious subject! Such behavior may get an immediate and furious response from the throne.

> A king delights in a wise servant, but a shameful servant incurs his wrath. (Proverbs 14:35)

Cowper was right about another thing in his hymn. God *is* his own interpreter. It seems that when people read the Bible they inevitably get the wrong impression from it; that's probably because sinful nature naturally recoils from a holy God and tries to twist the text into supporting lies about God. But when God speaks in the Word, through his Spirit, he calms the rebellion in the heart and "gives us a heart of flesh" that's more willing to *listen,* not doubt. He opens the eyes of the blind and opens the ears to hear.

> I will give you a new heart and put a new spirit in you; I will remove from you your heart of stone and give you a heart of flesh. And I will put my Spirit in you and **move you** to follow my decrees and be careful to keep my laws. (Ezekiel 36:26-27)

Conclusion

There *is* one sort of proof that the Bible offers for itself. Jesus mentioned it in the Gospels:

> Believe me when I say that I am in the Father and the Father is in me; or at least believe on the evidence of the miracles themselves. (John 14:11)

The idea is that Jesus did things that the Jews knew only God could do. Only God can raise the dead, only God can calm storms with a word. And here is a man (or so he seems!) doing these great works right in front of their eyes. Shouldn't that make us wonder whether his claims – that he's the Son of God, that he's the Savior, that he is the only way to Heaven, that his death will cleanse our souls from sin – might be true after all? The writer of Hebrews also alerts us to the same fact.

> We must pay more careful attention, therefore, to what we have heard, so that we do not drift away. For if the message spoken by angels was binding, and every violation and disobedience received its just punishment, how shall we escape if we ignore such a great salvation? This salvation, which was first announced by the Lord, was confirmed to us by those who heard him. God also testified to it by signs, wonders and various miracles, and gifts of the Holy Spirit distributed according to his will. (Hebrews 2:1-4)

The miracles showed people that they weren't dealing with an ordinary man; his claim of being from Heaven rang true when he did divine works. Jesus reminded those who were following his ministry that the Old Testament (Isaiah 61:1-3) predicted that the Holy One would someday come to earth, and everyone would know him by the amazing miracles he did.

> When the men came to Jesus, they said, "John the Baptist sent us to you to ask, 'Are you the one who was to come, or should we expect someone else?' " At that very time Jesus cured many who had diseases, sicknesses and evil spirits, and gave sight to many who were blind. So he replied to the messengers, "Go back and report to John what you have seen and heard: The blind receive sight, the lame walk, those who have leprosy are cured, the deaf hear, the dead are raised, and the good news is preached to the poor. Blessed is the man who does not fall away on account of me." (Luke 7:20-23)

But Jesus also knew that miracles – though impressive – don't necessarily convince people. We can be pretty stubborn in our unbelief when sin is at stake! The rich man, who found out the hard way that there really is a place of eternal torment for the soul, pleaded with Abraham to send someone to warn his family about it.

> He answered, 'Then I beg you, father, send Lazarus to my father's house, for I have five brothers. Let him warn them, so that they will not also come to this place of torment.' Abraham replied, 'They have Moses and the Prophets; let them listen to them.' 'No, father Abraham,' he said, 'but if someone from the dead goes to them, they will repent.' He said to him, 'If they do not listen to Moses and the Prophets, they will not be

convinced even if someone rises from the dead.' (Luke 16:27-31)

Notice the approach that Jesus prefers to take: simply tell people the truth. Very little else will convince them that it *is* the truth. They will either believe (if God opens their eyes) or they won't. Remember that the Pharisees saw the miracles of Christ, and they resolutely refused to believe. Well, they believe now!

Usually the Lord was content to declare his Word and let the sheep and the goats line up accordingly. Unbelief was not rewarded with pleadings and arguments from a frustrated God. Consider the example of Elijah. The Israelites were convinced that there was such a god as Baal, and they were no longer following the Lord. The time had come to show them that only Israel's God was God. When everyone showed up at Mt. Carmel for the showdown, they got more than they bargained for.

> "Answer me, O LORD, answer me, so these people will know that you, O LORD, are God, and that you are turning their hearts back again." Then the fire of the LORD fell and burned up the sacrifice, the wood, the stones and the soil, and also licked up the water in the trench. When all the people saw this, they fell prostrate and cried, "The LORD – he is God! The LORD – he is God!" Then Elijah commanded them, "Seize the prophets of Baal. Don't let anyone get away!" They seized them, and Elijah had them brought down to the Kishon Valley and slaughtered there. (1 Kings 18:37-40)

Unbelief is rewarded with punishment.

Those who believe God's Word, however, are rewarded with firstfruits of the life to come. They are brought out of darkness into light (so that they can see and know the world of

God), they are freed from the power of sin in their hearts, they are filled with peace and joy, they walk the way of holiness and righteousness, they hate wickedness and perversion, they love justice. (We're talking about real Christians, not the ones who claim the name but do not have the Holy Spirit in their hearts). Though the world doesn't like us, they have to admit that we have something that they don't have.

> Live such good lives among the pagans that, though they accuse you of doing wrong, they may see your good deeds and glorify God on the day he visits us. (2 Peter 2:12)

There is no denying the power of the Bible to save sinners, because it happens all the time in many people. That's the modern miracle that "proves" the Bible is really what it says it is.

> Now that you have purified yourselves by obeying the truth so that you have sincere love for your brothers, love one another deeply, from the heart. For you have been born again, not of perishable seed, but of imperishable, through the living and enduring Word of God. For, "All men are like grass, and all their glory is like the flowers of the field; the grass withers and the flowers fall, but the Word of the Lord stands forever." And this is the Word that was preached to you. (1 Peter 1:22-25)

Notes

Notes

www.ingramcontent.com/pod-product-compliance
Lightning Source LLC
Chambersburg PA
CBHW020018050426
42450CB00005B/534